Copyright 2020 Spiritual Gifts©
All rights reserved.

All rights reserved. No part of this book may be reproduced, stored in a retrieval system or transmitted, in amy form or by any means, electronic, mechanical, photocopying or otherwise without the permission of the publisher.

INSTRUCTIONS

 Turn off your distractions. Relax and enjoy the spirit of the quotes and the peaceful nature of the pictures.

 Have fun! There is no wrong way to color, and with this book you are sure to have hours of relaxation and enjoyment, with the added benefit of inspiring quotes from the scriptures.

 This book works best with color pencils or markers. Wet mediums might bleed through. As images are printed one side only, you may place a piece of paper or card if you notice bleed through.

Ask and it shall be given you,
seek and ye shall find
knock, and it shall be opened unto you.
Luke 11:9

For everyone who exalts himself will be humbled, and everyone who humbles himself will be exalted.
Luke 14:11

Therefore do not be anxious about tomorrow, for tomorrow will be anxious for itself. Sufficient for the day is its own trouble. - Matthew 6:34

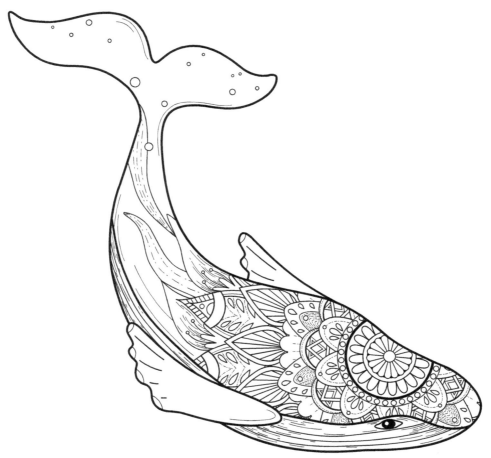

And he saith unto them, Follow me, and I will make you fishers of men. - Matthew 4:19

A new commandment I give unto you, That ye love one another: as I have loved you, that ye also love one another.
John 13:34

For the Son of Man came to seek and to save the lost.
Luke 19:10

Yea rather, blessed are they that hear the word of God, and keep it.
Luke 11:28

And why take ye thought for raiment? Consider the lilies of the field, how they grow; they toil not, neither do they spin: And yet I say unto you, That even Solomon in all his glory was not arrayed like one of these.
Matthew 6:28-29

Come unto me, all ye that labour and are heavy laden, and I will give you rest.
Matthew 11:28

Take my yoke upon you, and learn of me; for I am meek and lowly in heart: and ye shall find rest unto your souls.

Matthew 11:29

Printed in the USA
CPSIA information can be obtained
at www.ICGtesting.com
LVHW080008051224
798213LV00006B/837